The Power of Sales
Referrals

Unlocking a Powerful Growth Engine!

Gerard Assey

The Power of Sales Referrals
By
Gerard Assey
© Copyright 2023 by Author

Publishing Agency:
Collection Skills
19/18, Palli Arasan Street
Anna Nagar East
Chennai - 600 102

ISBN: 978-93-92492-67-9

(Image courtesy Freepik on https://www.freepik.com- Thank You)

Contents

Preface

Welcome to **'The Power of Sales Referrals:** *Unlocking A Powerful Growth Engine.'*
In today's competitive business landscape, where customers are constantly bombarded with marketing messages, sales professionals face the formidable challenge of breaking through the noise and building trust with their prospects. Amidst this struggle, sales referrals emerge as a beacon of hope- a powerful and proven method for driving business growth.

Referrals have long been recognized as a valuable source of new business. They harness the innate power of word-of-mouth marketing, leveraging the trust and credibility that comes from a personal recommendation. When satisfied customers and trusted partners enthusiastically refer your products or services, they become your advocates, effectively vouching for your business. And this word-of-mouth advertising is the best means of advertising. Look at some of these examples:

How often do we ask someone to recommend a good hotel or restaurant in a particular locality?

When someone asks for feedback on where to buy a car or get it repaired, don't we answer based on our personal experiences?

One of the most effective ways to build trust with new clients is by being introduced by a mutually trusted party. Referrals can make a huge difference in your overall sales during a year. Consider the impact of being able to generate just one referral each week. This will work out to 50 new clients each year, even after you take a 2 week vacation. Now imagine if you were to get one per day! The point is that you can earn more money without working additional hours or shifts and without working harder. Your closing ratios will be much higher with these referrals, as you will now enjoy a certain level of trust with these new prospects. You will find yourself dealing with warm leads as opposed to cold ones. People are more likely to trust an advisor whom they hear about from a trustworthy friend, family member, or colleague, and customers will be more likely to accept your feedback, suggestions, and ideas, because one of their friends or relatives has recommended you. Clients' satisfaction is the best proof of your professional qualities. Encourage your past or current satisfied clients to recommend you to others. Encouraging referrals is a great way to take advantage of word-of-mouth strategy and build trust with prospects without breaking the bank. The more referrals you ask for, the more business you will get. Recognize that referrals can generate additional revenue, without you having to work harder.

This book is therefore a comprehensive guide that aims to unveil the untapped potential of sales referrals and provide you with the strategies, techniques, and insights necessary to harness this super power. Whether you are a seasoned sales professional seeking to revitalize your approach or an entrepreneur looking to leverage referrals as a growth engine, this book will equip you with the knowledge and tools needed to unlock a new level of sales success.

In the following chapters, we will explore the multifaceted nature of sales referrals, delving into the art and science behind this age-old practice. We will examine the tangible benefits that referrals bring, from increased conversion rates and shorter sales cycles to elevated customer loyalty and lifetime value. Moreover, we will delve into the psychology that underlies referral-based selling, understanding why people are more likely to trust a recommendation from someone they know and how we can leverage this human inclination to our advantage.

Building upon this foundation, we will move to how to cultivate a referral mindset—a fundamental shift in perspectives that encourages you to view referrals as an integral part of your sales strategy. We will cover the importance of creating a referral-worthy business that consistently exceeds customer expectations and fosters strong relationships. You will learn how to identify and nurture your most valuable referral sources, building trust and rapport with individuals and organizations that are invested in your success.

Asking for referrals is an art in itself, and we will provide you with practical techniques and proven strategies to confidently seek referrals from your satisfied clients and strategic partners, while addressing common objections and challenges along the way, and equipping you with the tools to overcome them and master the art of the referral ask. Additionally, this book gets into the role of technology in the referral process. We will discuss how to leverage customer relationship management (CRM) systems, social media platforms, and automation tools to streamline your referral generation efforts, enhancing efficiency and scalability.

Measuring and scaling referral success is a crucial aspect of any referral program, and we will guide you through the key metrics and evaluation techniques that will help you track your progress and optimize your referral strategy. We will also tackle common challenges and obstacles, providing insights and solutions to address skepticism and resistance while maximizing the effectiveness of your referral efforts.

Finally, we will delve into the future of referral-based selling, exploring emerging trends, technologies, and customer behaviors. By understanding the evolving landscape, you will be empowered to adapt your strategies and stay ahead of the curve.

Throughout this book, you will find practical examples, case studies, and actionable steps that bring the concepts to life along with sample referral request scripts and templates, to help you further

Now, it's time to embark on this journey that will transform your sales approach and unlock the boundless potential of sales referrals. By the end of this book, you will possess the knowledge and strategies needed to build a thriving referral network, supercharge your sales results, and create sustainable growth for your business. Let's begin our exploration of **'The Power of Sales Referrals.'**

An Understanding of Sales Referrals (Concept, Impact, Psychology)

Let us first start by having an understanding of the basics of Sales Referrals. We will begin by:

Understanding the concept of sales referrals: Sales referrals, at their core, involve the act of leveraging existing relationships and networks to obtain introductions and recommendations from satisfied customers, clients, or strategic partners. It is the process of harnessing the power of word-of-mouth marketing to generate new business opportunities. Referrals can come in various forms, such as personal recommendations, testimonials, or online reviews.

Example 1: Sarah, a satisfied customer of a software company, recommends the company's product to her colleague, Jonathan, who is in need of similar software. Sarah's referral provides an introduction and a positive testimonial, influencing Jonathan's decision to consider the recommended software.

Example 2: A financial advisor builds strong relationships with their clients over time. Through these relationships, clients become advocates and refer friends, family members, or colleagues who may benefit from financial planning services. These referrals open up new avenues for the financial advisor to expand their client base.

The impact of referrals on business growth: Referrals have a profound impact on business growth, yielding several significant advantages over traditional marketing and lead generation methods.

Enhanced Trust and Credibility: Referrals inherently carry a high level of trust and credibility because they come from trusted sources within the prospect's network. People are more likely to trust recommendations from individuals they know and respect, making referrals a powerful tool for establishing initial trust with potential customers.

Example 1: When looking for a reliable contractor, John trusts the recommendation of his neighbor, who had a positive experience with a contractor during their home renovation project. Based on this referral, John is more likely to choose the recommended contractor over other options.

Higher Conversion Rates and Shorter Sales Cycles: Referrals often result in higher conversion rates and shorter sales cycles. Prospects that come through referrals are already pre-qualified and more receptive to the sales message, making it easier to move them through the sales process quickly.

Example 2: A software sales representative receives a referral from an existing client. The referred prospect, having heard positive things about the software, is already interested and more likely to convert into a paying customer. This leads to a shorter sales cycle and a higher likelihood of closing the deal.

Increased Customer Lifetime Value: Referral-based customers tend to have higher lifetime value due to their higher levels of satisfaction, loyalty, and engagement. They are more likely to become repeat customers and refer others in turn, creating a cycle of continuous growth and customer advocacy.

Example 3: A fitness trainer receives a referral from a satisfied client who had great results. The referred client not only becomes a long-term customer but also refers their friends to the trainer's services. As a result, the trainer's customer base expands, generating increased revenue and an extended customer lifetime value.

The psychology behind referral-based selling: Referral-based selling operates on various psychological principles that influence how individuals perceive and act upon referrals.

Social Proof and Influence: People are heavily influenced by the actions and opinions of others. When individuals see their peers recommending a product or service, they are more likely to perceive it as valuable and trustworthy, leading to an increased likelihood of making a purchase.

Example 1: A restaurant receives positive online reviews and testimonials from satisfied customers. These reviews serve as social proof, influencing potential diners to choose the restaurant over its competitors.

Reciprocity and Gratitude: When someone receives a referral or recommendation, they often feel a sense of gratitude and reciprocity towards the referrer. This emotional response can motivate individuals to reciprocate the favor by providing referrals or other forms of support.

Example 2: A graphic designer receives a referral from a fellow designer who was unable to take on a new project. In gratitude, the designer refers their own clients to the fellow designer when their workload permits, establishing a mutually beneficial referral exchange.

Trust and Risk Reduction: Referrals help reduce perceived risks for potential customers. By receiving recommendations from trusted sources, individuals feel more comfortable making purchasing decisions, knowing they are less likely to encounter negative experiences or wasted investments.

Example 3: A prospective homeowner is looking for a reputable real estate agent to assist them with their property search. They receive a referral from a trusted friend who recently purchased a home. The referral reduces the perceived risk and uncertainty associated with choosing a real estate agent, increasing the likelihood of engaging the referred agent's services.

By understanding the concept of sales referrals, recognizing their impact on business growth, and unraveling the psychology behind referral-based selling, sales professionals can harness the full potential of referrals to achieve sustainable growth and success. In the subsequent chapters, we will delve deeper into the strategies and techniques necessary to generate and maximize sales referrals.

The Benefits of Sales Referrals

From enhanced trust and credibility to higher conversion rates and increased customer lifetime value, referrals offer a wealth of advantages that can drive substantial growth and success.

Here are ten benefits of sales referrals with specific examples for each:

1. Enhanced Trust and Credibility: Referrals create a higher level of trust and credibility for your business, as prospects are more likely to trust recommendations from people they know. For example, if a friend refers a restaurant and shares their positive experience, you're more likely to trust their recommendation and try the restaurant yourself.

2. Higher Conversion Rates and Shorter Sales Cycles: Referrals have a higher conversion rate compared to other leads. When someone is referred to your business, they already have a level of trust and are more likely to convert into a customer. This leads to shorter sales cycles and faster revenue generation. For instance, a referred prospect for a software service is more likely to convert into a paying customer compared to a cold lead.

3. Increased Customer Lifetime Value: Referred customers tend to have a higher customer lifetime value (CLV) compared to other acquisition channels. They often become loyal customers and are more likely to make repeat purchases. For example, a customer who was referred to a clothing brand may become a

loyal customer, making regular purchases and referring more friends.

4. Cost-Effective Customer Acquisition: Referrals can significantly lower your customer acquisition costs. Since you're leveraging existing relationships, the cost of acquiring a new customer through referrals is often lower compared to traditional marketing and advertising channels. This helps improve your bottom line. A referral-based car dealership can save on marketing expenses by relying on satisfied customers to refer their friends and family.

5. Higher Quality Leads: Referrals tend to bring higher quality leads, as they are pre-qualified and more likely to have a genuine interest in your products or services. For instance, if a business owner is referred to an accounting firm by a trusted colleague, they are more likely to be in need of accounting services and have a higher chance of becoming a valuable client.

6. Expanded Network and Reach: Referrals provide an opportunity to tap into new networks and reach potential customers who may not have been aware of your business otherwise. When your customers refer their connections, it allows you to extend your reach and access new markets. For example, if a software company receives a referral from a client in a different industry, it opens the door to expand customer base in that industry.

7. Personalized Recommendations and Targeted Marketing: Referrals allow for personalized recommendations based on the needs and

preferences of the referred prospect. When someone refers a specific product or service to a friend, they can highlight its relevance to that person's specific requirements. This targeted approach increases the likelihood of conversion. For instance, a referred prospect for a fitness app may receive personalized recommendations on workout routines based on their goals and fitness level.

8. Positive Brand Advocacy and Word-of-Mouth Marketing: Referrals turn satisfied customers into brand advocates who promote your business through word-of-mouth marketing. These advocates can spread positive reviews and recommendations to their networks, creating a ripple effect of awareness and interest. For example, when a customer raves about their experience with a mobile phone provider and recommends it to their friends, it generates positive buzz for the brand.

9. Increased Sales Opportunities: Referrals open doors to new sales opportunities that may have been challenging to access through traditional channels. When someone refers you to a potential customer, it creates a warm introduction and increases the chances of closing a sale. For instance, a referred prospect for a B2B software solution may be more willing to schedule a sales meeting compared to a cold outreach.

10. Long-Term Business Growth and Sustainability: A strong referral program fosters continuous business growth and sustainability. By consistently generating referrals and leveraging customer

relationships, your business can experience steady growth and a sustainable customer base. This can lead to long-term success. An insurance agency that focuses on building strong referral partnerships with local real estate agents can experience continuous growth and a stable stream of new clients.

These benefits highlight the immense value that sales referrals bring to a business. By leveraging referrals, you can enhance trust, increase conversions, reduce costs, and foster long-term relationships, ultimately driving business growth and success.

Building a Referral-Driven Mindset and Culture

In this chapter, we will explore the importance of building a referral mindset- a fundamental shift in perspective that allows sales professionals and organizations to recognize the value and potential of referrals. We will cover how to have a mind-set and cultivate a culture of referrals within your organization; overcome common misconceptions and objections, thereby embracing referrals as a powerful driver of business growth.

Shifting your perspective on sales and referrals: To truly harness the power of referrals, it is essential to shift your perspective on sales and recognize the significance of referrals as a strategic and integral part of your sales process. Embracing referrals requires acknowledging that they are not simply a byproduct of successful business interactions but rather a deliberate and proactive approach to generating new opportunities.

Traditionally, sales professionals may view their primary role as closing deals and generating revenue. However, by shifting their perspective to include referrals as a core objective, they recognize that every satisfied customer or client has the potential to become a valuable advocate who can contribute to their long-term success. This shift in mindset allows sales professionals to approach their interactions with customers and clients with a focus on building strong relationships that foster referral opportunities.

Cultivating a culture of referrals within your organization: Building a culture of referrals involves creating an environment where every member of your organization recognizes the importance of referrals and actively participates in referral generation efforts. This culture permeates across all departments and levels, fostering a collective commitment to providing exceptional customer experiences and actively seeking referral opportunities.

As an example: A financial services firm understands the power of referrals and cultivates a culture of referrals within its organization. The firm regularly communicates the importance of referrals to all employees, provides training on effective referral strategies, and celebrates referral successes. Every team member, from advisors to support staff, is encouraged to prioritize client satisfaction and actively seek opportunities to generate referrals. This collective commitment to referrals becomes an integral part of the firm's identity and fuels its growth.

Key steps to building a Referral driven culture in the organization

Building a referral-driven culture in an organization requires a strategic and systematic approach. Here are some steps to help you establish and nurture a referral-driven culture, along with specific examples:

1. Set Clear Expectations: Clearly communicate the importance of referrals and their role in business growth to all employees. Establish referral goals and make them part of the performance metrics. For example, during team meetings, emphasize the significance of referrals and share success stories of employees who have contributed to the referral program.

2. Provide Training and Resources: Educate employees on the value of referrals, how to identify referral opportunities, and how to make effective referral requests. Conduct training sessions and provide resources such as referral scripts, email templates, and collateral that employees can use to promote the referral program. For instance, conduct role-playing exercises to help employees practice making referral requests in different scenarios.
3. Recognize and Reward Referral Success: Implement a reward and recognition system to motivate employees to actively participate in the referral program. Recognize and publicly acknowledge employees who generate successful referrals, either through monetary rewards, incentives, or non-monetary recognition like employee of the month awards. For example, create a 'Referral Leader Board' that showcases the top referrers within the organization.
4. Foster Collaboration and Knowledge Sharing: Encourage employees to collaborate and share referral strategies and success stories with their peers. Create platforms for employees to discuss and exchange best practices. For instance, organize regular team meetings or online forums where employees can share their referral experiences, challenges, and strategies.
5. Integrate Referral Opportunities into Workflows: Integrate referral opportunities into the daily workflows and processes of employees. Identify touch points in customer

interactions where referrals can be naturally introduced. For example, after a successful project completion, encourage employees to ask clients for referrals by expressing gratitude for their satisfaction and asking if they know anyone else who could benefit from the company's services.

6. Track and Measure Referral Performance: Implement a system to track and measure referral activities and outcomes. Monitor referral conversion rates, track the number of referrals generated by each employee, and assess the quality of referred leads. Use this data to identify areas of improvement and recognize top performers. For example, utilize customer relationship management (CRM) software to track referral activities and outcomes.

7. Celebrate Referral Success Stories: Share success stories of referred clients and the positive impact they have had on the organization. Highlight how referrals have contributed to the growth and success of the company. Celebrate these stories through internal communications, company newsletters, or social media. For instance, feature testimonials or case studies from referred clients, showcasing how their referrals have made a difference.

8. Continuously Improve and Optimize: Regularly review and analyze the effectiveness of the referral program. Collect feedback from employees and clients to identify areas for improvement. Adjust strategies, processes, and incentives based on feedback and market

dynamics. For example, conduct surveys or feedback sessions to gather insights on the referral program's effectiveness and implement changes accordingly.

9. Provide Ongoing Support and Guidance: Offer ongoing support and guidance to employees to help them succeed in generating referrals. Assign referral program champions or mentors who can provide guidance, answer questions, and share best practices. Provide resources such as updated referral materials and ongoing training sessions to keep employees engaged and informed.

10. Lead by Example: As a leader, actively participate in the referral program and demonstrate your commitment to referrals. Lead by example by making referral requests yourself and sharing success stories within the organization. Your involvement and enthusiasm will inspire employees to follow suit.

Building a referral-driven culture takes time and effort, but with these steps, organizations can create a culture where referrals are valued, celebrated, and integrated into the fabric of the business.

Creating a Referral-Worthy Business

By focusing on delivering exceptional products or services, providing outstanding customer experiences, and developing strong relationships with existing clients, you can lay the foundation for generating a steady stream of valuable referrals.

Delivering exceptional products or services: To become referral-worthy, your business must strive to deliver products or services that consistently exceed customer expectations. By providing exceptional quality, value, and innovation, you create a strong foundation for customer satisfaction and advocacy.

Example: A graphic design agency sets itself apart by consistently producing visually stunning and creative designs that align with clients' visions and brand identities. The agency's commitment to excellence ensures that each client receives a final product that exceeds their expectations, making them more likely to refer the agency to others in need of design services.

Providing outstanding customer experiences: Alongside exceptional products or services, creating outstanding customer experiences is crucial for fostering positive word-of-mouth and generating referrals. Every interaction with your customers should be marked by attentiveness, responsiveness, and a personalized approach.

Example: A luxury hotel focuses on providing unforgettable experiences to its guests. From the warm welcome at check-in to the personalized concierge services and attention to detail throughout the stay, the hotel creates an atmosphere of exceptional hospitality. Guests who receive outstanding experiences are more likely to share their positive experiences with friends, family, and colleagues, leading to valuable referrals for the hotel.

Developing strong relationships with existing clients: Building strong relationships with your existing clients is key to generating referrals. By cultivating trust, demonstrating genuine care, and consistently adding value, you transform clients into advocates who willingly refer your business to their networks.

Example: A marketing consultant invests time and effort in building relationships with their clients. They regularly check in with clients to understand their evolving needs, provide valuable insights and recommendations, and go the extra mile to ensure client success. As a result, clients not only appreciate the consultant's expertise but also feel a sense of loyalty and reciprocity, leading them to refer the consultant to other businesses seeking marketing guidance.

By delivering exceptional products or services, providing outstanding customer experiences, and developing strong relationships with existing clients, your business becomes a referral-worthy entity. In the following chapters, we will delve into specific strategies and techniques that will help you actively seek and leverage referrals, amplifying the impact of your referral-worthy business and driving sustainable growth.

Identifying and Nurturing Referral Sources

We will now explore the process of identifying and nurturing referral sources- with individuals or organizations who have the potential to become valuable advocates and consistently refer business to you. By understanding your ideal referral sources, employing techniques for identifying potential advocates, and building strong relationships with referral partners, you can create a robust network of referral sources to fuel your business growth.

Understanding your ideal referral sources: To effectively generate referrals, it is important to have a clear understanding of your ideal referral sources. These are individuals or entities who have direct or indirect access to your target market and can endorse your products or services to potential customers. Understanding the characteristics and traits of your ideal referral sources allows you to focus your efforts on cultivating relationships with those who are most likely to generate quality referrals.

Example: A web development agency identifies that their ideal referral sources are marketing agencies who often work with clients in need of website redesign or development. These agencies have existing relationships with potential clients and can refer them to the web development agency. By focusing on building relationships with marketing agencies, the web development agency increases their chances of receiving high-quality referrals.

Identifying potential advocates: Once you have a clear understanding of your ideal referral sources, it is essential to employ techniques for identifying potential advocates within those sources. This involves proactive research, networking, and leveraging existing connections to uncover individuals or organizations who are likely to refer business to you.

Example: A personal trainer looking to expand their client base identifies that local nutritionists and doctors could be potential advocates. They attend networking events and industry conferences to connect with professionals in these fields. Through conversations and relationship-building, the personal trainer discovers nutritionists and doctors who are passionate about holistic health and wellness. These professionals become potential advocates who can refer clients seeking a comprehensive approach to their well-being.

Key Techniques for identifying potential advocates for referrals

1. Customer Satisfaction Surveys: Use customer satisfaction surveys to identify satisfied customers who are likely to become advocates. Look for customers who provide positive feedback, high ratings, or express a willingness to recommend your business. For example, a software company may include a question in their survey asking customers if they would recommend the product to others.

2. Net Promoter Score (NPS): Implement the Net Promoter Score system to identify customers who are likely to refer others. Customers who give high NPS scores are potential advocates. Reach out to them and ask for referrals. For instance, a telecommunications provider may identify customers with a high NPS and

proactively ask if they would be willing to refer their friends or family.

3. Social Media Listening: Monitor social media platforms for customers who mention positive experiences with your business. Engage with these customers and build relationships with them. These customers are often willing to refer others. For example, a clothing retailer might come across a tweet from a customer expressing their love for a recent purchase. The retailer can reach out to that customer and explore the possibility of referrals.

4. Online Reviews and Testimonials: Pay attention to online reviews and testimonials from customers who speak highly of your products or services. Reach out to these customers and ask if they would be open to referring others. For instance, a hotel might identify business guests who leave positive reviews on travel review websites and follow up with them to discuss potential referrals.

5. Referral Tracking Systems: Utilize referral tracking systems or software to identify customers who have previously referred others. These customers have already demonstrated their willingness to advocate for your business. Engage with them and explore opportunities for ongoing referrals. For example, an e-commerce platform can track customer referrals and offer incentives to top referrers.

6. Customer Interactions and Feedback: Pay attention to customer interactions and feedback to identify individuals who show a high level of enthusiasm and engagement with

your business. These customers are more likely to refer others. Engage in conversations with them and explore the possibility of referrals. For instance, a fitness center might notice a member who actively participates in classes, provides feedback, and engages with instructors. This member could be a potential advocate for referrals.

7. Industry Influencers and Thought Leaders: Identify influential individuals within your industry who can become advocates for your business. Engage with these influencers, build relationships, and explore collaboration opportunities. They can refer their followers to your products or services. For example, a skincare brand might partner with a popular beauty blogger who can refer their audience to the brand's products.

8. Networking Events and Trade Shows: Attend networking events and trade shows related to your industry to connect with potential advocates. Engage in conversations, showcase your expertise, and build relationships. These individuals can become valuable referral sources. For instance, a digital marketing agency attending a marketing conference might connect with attendees who are interested in their services and could potentially refer others.

9. Existing Business Partners and Suppliers: Explore potential referral partnerships with your existing business partners and suppliers. They have a vested interest in your success and may be willing to refer their clients or contacts to your business. Engage in

conversations and discuss mutual referral opportunities. For example, a graphic design agency might partner with a printing company to refer clients to each other's services.

10. Employee Advocacy: Encourage and empower your employees to become advocates for your business. They have personal networks that can be leveraged for referrals. Implement an employee referral program and provide incentives for their referrals. For example, an IT consulting firm can incentivize employees to refer potential clients from their professional networks.

These techniques can help you identify potential advocates for referrals and expand your network of referral sources. By leveraging these relationships, you can tap into new customer bases

Building and maintaining relationships with referral partners: Building strong relationships with referral partners is crucial for nurturing a network of advocates who consistently refer business to you. It involves establishing trust, demonstrating value, and maintaining regular communication to stay top of mind. Additionally, it is essential to reciprocate and provide support to your referral partners whenever possible.

Example: A real estate agent understands the importance of building relationships with referral partners such as mortgage brokers, home inspectors, and interior designers. The real estate agent meets with these professionals to understand their services and expertise better. They maintain regular communication, share industry insights, and provide referrals for complementary services whenever they come across potential clients. By nurturing these relationships, the real estate agent creates a network of referral partners who reciprocate by referring clients in need of real estate services.

By understanding your ideal referral sources, employing techniques to identify potential advocates, and building strong relationships with referral partners, you can create a network of reliable referral sources. In the subsequent chapters, we will cover specific strategies and tactics that will empower you to effectively engage and leverage your referral sources, maximizing the referral potential of your network.

The Art of Asking for Referrals

Asking for referrals is a crucial skill that allows you to proactively seek and leverage referral opportunities. Mastering the art of asking for referrals will enable you to tap into the full potential of your network and generate valuable business opportunities.

Timing and strategies for asking for referrals: Timing plays a crucial role in the success of your referral ask. It is important to choose the right moment when your customer or client is most satisfied with your products or services. Additionally, employing effective strategies can enhance your chances of receiving a positive response to your referral request.

Example: A freelance photographer completes a photo-shoot session for a client's wedding. The client expresses immense satisfaction with the photographs and expresses gratitude for capturing their special moments beautifully. Sensing the peak of customer satisfaction, the photographer seizes the opportunity to ask for referrals by saying, *"I'm thrilled that you loved the photos! If you know anyone else who is looking for a skilled photographer for their special occasions, I would greatly appreciate it if you could refer them to me."*

Crafting effective referral requests: Crafting an effective referral request involves being clear, concise, and compelling in your message. You want to make it easy for your customers or clients to understand what you are asking for and why it would benefit them and the referred party.

Example: A financial advisor reaches out to a long-term client who recently achieved their financial goals with the advisor's guidance. In the referral request, the advisor says, *"I'm delighted to see you successfully reach your financial milestones. If you have friends or family members who could benefit from expert financial planning and guidance like you have, I would be grateful for any introductions. As a thank you, I'm offering a complimentary financial review for any referrals you send my way."*

Here are sample referral request scripts and templates that you as a starting point when asking for referrals:

Template 1: General Referral Request Email

Subject: *Request for Referrals*

Hi [Client/Contact's Name],

I hope this email finds you well. I wanted to reach out and ask if you could help me with something. As a valued client/partner of [Your Company], you have firsthand experience with our products/services, and your opinion holds great weight.

I'm reaching out to see if you know anyone in your network who could benefit from [Briefly describe your products/services]. If you could provide an introduction or refer them to me, I would be truly grateful.

Thank you for your continued support, and I appreciate any assistance you can provide. Feel free to reach out if you have any questions or need further information.

Best regards, [Your Name]

Template 2: Referral Request Script for a Phone Call

[Your Name]: Hi [Client/Contact's Name], it's [Your Name] from [Your Company]. I hope you're doing

well. I wanted to ask if you could help me with a favor please. As a satisfied client/partner, your opinion means a lot to us. Do you happen to know anyone in your network who might benefit from [Briefly describe your products/services]? If you could provide an introduction or refer them to me, it would be greatly appreciated.

Template 3: Referral Request Script for a Face-to-Face Meeting

[Your Name]: [Client/Contact's Name], it's great to see you! I wanted to catch up and also ask if you could help me with a small favor please. Given your experience with [Your Company], I thought you might know someone who could benefit from [Briefly describe your products/services]. If you could make an introduction or refer them to me, I would be extremely grateful.

Template 4: Referral Request Script for Social Media

Hi [Client/Contact's Name],
I hope you're doing well! I wanted to reach out and ask for your help. As someone who has experienced the value of [Your Company]'s products/services, your recommendations carry weight. If you know anyone in your network who could benefit from [Briefly describe your products/services], I would greatly appreciate it if you could tag them in the comments or send them my way.
Thanks in advance for your support! [Your Name]

Template 5: Referral Request Script for LinkedIn
Hi [Client/Contact's Name],

I hope you're doing well. I wanted to reach out and ask if you could help me with something. As a valued connection on LinkedIn, I believe you understand the value of professional networks. If you know anyone in your network who could benefit from [Briefly describe your products/services], I would be grateful if you could introduce us or provide a referral.

Thank you for your support! [Your Name]

Template 6: Referral Request Script for a Follow-up Email

Subject: Quick Favor to Ask

Hi [Client/Contact's Name],

I hope you're doing well. I wanted to follow up on our recent conversation and ask if you could do me a quick favor. As someone who has experienced the value of [Your Company]'s products/services, your referrals could make a significant impact.

If you know anyone in your network who might be interested in [Briefly describe your products/services], I would greatly appreciate it if you could provide an introduction or refer them to me.

Thank you for your support, and I look forward to hearing from you.

Best regards, [Your Name]

Template 7: Referral Request Script for a Personalized Email

Subject: Your Feedback and Referrals are Valued

Hi [Client/Contact's Name],

I hope this email finds you well. I wanted to take a moment to express my gratitude for your continued support and partnership with [Your Company]. Your feedback has been invaluable in helping us improve our products/services.

I wanted to reach out and ask if you know anyone in your network who could benefit from [Briefly describe your products/services]. Your personal recommendation would mean a lot to me, and I would be thrilled if you could provide an introduction or refer them to me.

Thank you for your time, and I appreciate your support.

Warm regards, [Your Name]

Template 8: Referral Request Script for a Thank You Card

Dear [Client/Contact's Name],

I wanted to take a moment to express my heartfelt thanks for your trust in our products/services and your ongoing support. Your satisfaction is our top priority.

If you have any friends, colleagues, or business associates who could benefit from [Briefly describe your products/services], I would be extremely grateful if you could refer them to us. Your personal recommendation holds great weight, and I would be honored to serve those within your network.

Once again, thank you for your continued support, and please let me know if there's anything I can do for you.

With sincere appreciation, [Your Name]

Template 9: Referral Request Script for a Follow-up Call

[Your Name]: Hi [Client/Contact's Name], it's [Your Name] from [Your Company]. I hope you're doing well. I wanted to reach out and see if you could help me with something. As someone who has been pleased with our products/services, I wanted to ask if

you know anyone in your network who might benefit from [Briefly describe your products/services]. If you could provide an introduction or refer them to me, it would mean a lot.

Template 10: Referral Request Script for a Networking Event

[Your Name]: Hi [Client/Contact's Name], it's great to see you here! I wanted to catch up and also ask if you could assist me with something. Given your expertise and network, I thought you might know someone who could benefit from [Briefly describe your products/services]. If you could make an introduction or refer them to me, I would be extremely grateful.

You could modify these templates to align with your specific situation and relationship with the client or contact, by personalizing the message, making it genuine and showing appreciation for their support and the value they bring to your referral efforts. Remember, building and nurturing relationships is key to successful referral generation.

Overcoming fear and discomfort in the referral ask: Many individuals feel a fear or anxiety and are uncomfortable when asking for referrals due to concerns of being perceived as pushy or imposing. Overcoming these barriers requires a mindset shift and reframing the referral ask as an opportunity to provide value and help others.

Misconceptions and objections can hinder the adoption of a referral mindset. It is important to address and overcome these obstacles to fully embrace the potential of referrals. Common misconceptions include concerns about asking for referrals, the belief that referrals happen organically without proactive effort, or the fear of jeopardizing existing relationships by seeking referrals. Sales professionals may feel uncomfortable asking for referrals, fearing that it may come across as pushy or self-serving. However, by reframing the referral ask as a way to provide value and benefit, to both, the referrer and the referred prospect, the sales professional can overcome this objection. By demonstrating how a referral benefits the referrer by helping their network access valuable solutions and services, the sales professional can approach the referral ask with confidence and authenticity.

Example: A sales representative experiences fear when asking a client for referrals, worried about jeopardizing the existing relationship. To overcome this fear, the sales representative adopts a customer-centric approach and focuses on the value they can provide to the referred prospects. They say something like, *"I've greatly enjoyed working with you and helping your business succeed. If you know of any other business owners who could benefit from our solutions and expertise, please let me know. I would love to provide them with the same level of support and results we've achieved together."*

Overcoming fear and discomfort in the asking for referrals

Overcoming fear and discomfort in asking for referrals can be challenging, but it's crucial for the success of your referral program. Here are ten strategies or ideas to help you overcome those barriers:

1. Develop a Referral Mindset: Shift your mindset and view asking for referrals as a natural part of building relationships and

growing your business. Remind yourself that satisfied customers and contacts would be happy to refer others if they believe in the value you provide.

2. Practice and Role Play: Practice asking for referrals with colleagues or friends to build confidence. Role-play different scenarios to simulate real-life situations. This will help you refine your approach and ease any discomfort you may have.

3. Start Small: Begin by asking for referrals from individuals you have a strong rapport with or those who have expressed satisfaction with your products or services. Starting with warm contacts will help you feel more at ease and increase the likelihood of receiving positive responses.

4. Offer Incentives: Consider providing incentives to both the referrer and the referred customer. Incentives can motivate you to overcome fear and encourage your customers and contacts to actively participate in the referral process. For example, offer discounts, exclusive access, or rewards for successful referrals.

5. Leverage Social Proof: Share success stories and testimonials from customers who have benefited from your products or services. Highlighting positive experiences can alleviate your fear and discomfort by demonstrating that others have had a positive outcome from referrals.

6. Use Referral Scripts or Templates: Prepare referral scripts or templates to guide your conversations. Having a structure and key talking points can provide a sense of

confidence and help you navigate the referral ask more smoothly. Customize these scripts based on your industry and target audience.

7. Focus on the Value Exchange: When asking for referrals, emphasize the value and benefits that the referral will receive. Highlight how your products or services can solve their problems or fulfill their needs. By focusing on the value exchange, you'll feel more comfortable making the ask.

8. Seek Internal Support: Discuss your concerns and challenges with colleagues or mentors who have experience with referrals. They can provide guidance, share their own experiences, and offer tips on overcoming fear and discomfort.

9. Celebrate Referral Success: Celebrate and acknowledge your referral successes. When you see the positive outcomes that come from asking for referrals, it can boost your confidence and reduce future fears. Share your referral successes with others, both internally and externally.

10. Track Your Referral Performance: Keep track of your referral performance and results. Monitor the number of referrals received and the conversions that resulted from them. Seeing tangible results can build confidence and reinforce the importance of asking for referrals.

Remember, overcoming fear and discomfort in asking for referrals is a process that takes time and practice. By implementing these strategies and consistently challenging yourself, you'll become more comfortable and confident in seeking referrals, leading to greater success for your business.

By understanding the timing and strategies for asking for referrals, crafting effective referral requests, and overcoming fear and discomfort in the referral ask, you can confidently seek and receive valuable referrals.

Maximizing Referral Conversions

We will now look at the strategies and techniques to maximize referral conversion—the process of turning referred prospects into satisfied customers, by covering the importance of qualifying and following up on referrals, leveraging personalization and tailored messaging, and strategies for overcoming common referral objections. By effectively managing and converting referrals, you can harness the full potential of your referral network and drive business growth.

Qualifying and following up on referrals: Qualifying referrals ensures that you invest your time and resources in pursuing the most promising opportunities. Following up on referrals in a timely and professional manner demonstrates your commitment to potential customers and increases the likelihood of conversion.

Example: A software development company receives a referral from a trusted partner. Before reaching out to the referred prospect, they conduct research to understand the prospect's industry, specific needs, and potential fit for their services. Armed with this information, they customize their approach and follow up with a personalized email that highlights how their expertise aligns with the prospect's business goals.

Leveraging personalization and tailored messaging: Personalization and tailored messaging are essential when engaging with referred prospects. By demonstrating that you understand their unique needs and challenges, you establish rapport and credibility, increasing the chances of conversion.

Example: A marketing agency receives a referral for a small e-commerce business seeking help with social media advertising. When reaching out to the referred prospect, they reference the specific challenges faced by e-commerce businesses and share success stories of similar clients they have worked with. This tailored messaging showcases their expertise in addressing the prospect's unique requirements and increases the likelihood of converting the referral into a client.

Strategies for overcoming common referral objections: Referral objections can arise due to various reasons, such as perceived risk, budget constraints, or a lack of understanding of your offerings. Overcoming these objections requires active listening, addressing concerns, and demonstrating the value and benefits of your products or services.

Example: A financial advisor receives a referral from a satisfied client, but the referred prospect expresses concerns about the potential costs and risks associated with financial investments. To overcome this objection, the financial advisor arranges a consultation where they listen attentively to the prospect's concerns and provide detailed explanations of their investment strategies, emphasizing the long-term benefits and potential returns. By addressing the objections and providing reassurance, the financial advisor can convert the referral into a new client.

Key Strategies for overcoming common referral objections

Overcoming objections is an essential skill when asking for referrals. Here are five key strategies to help you address common referral objections:

1. Provide Clear Value Proposition: Clearly communicate the value and benefits that the referred individual will receive by engaging with your products or services. Address objections by highlighting how you can solve their problems or fulfill their needs. For example, if someone objects by saying, *"I'm not sure if my friend would be interested,"* you can respond by saying, *"Our service has helped many people save time and money. Your friend might benefit from the same advantages."*

2. Offer Social Proof: Share testimonials, success stories, or case studies from satisfied customers who have received value from your business. Social proof provides credibility and helps overcome objections based on skepticism. For instance, if someone says, *"I'm not sure if it's worth it,"* you can reply by saying, *"Many of our customers have experienced significant results and have shared their positive feedback. Let me share a success story with you."*

3. Address Privacy and Trust Concerns: Assure individuals that their privacy and trust are respected. Emphasize that their referral will be handled professionally and that you value their relationship. For example, if someone objects by saying, *"I'm not comfortable sharing my friend's contact information,"* you can respond by saying, *"We take privacy seriously and will handle your friend's information with the utmost care. Rest assured that we will respect their privacy and only reach out with their permission."*

4. Offer Incentives or Rewards: Consider providing incentives or rewards to individuals who provide referrals. By offering an extra benefit, you can alleviate objections related to time or effort. For instance, if someone says, *"I don't have the time to think of anyone to refer,"* you can reply by saying, *"We appreciate your support. As a token of our gratitude, we offer a referral bonus for each successful referral you provide. It's a way for us to give back to you for your time and effort."*

5. Follow Up and Maintain Communication: Regularly follow up with individuals who express objections or reservations. By staying in touch, you can address any concerns, provide additional information, and build trust over time. For example, if someone says, *"I'll think about it,"* you can follow up by saying, *"I wanted to check in and see if you had any further questions or concerns about referring someone. I'm here to help and provide any additional information you may need."*

Remember, overcoming referral objections requires active listening, empathy, and providing relevant solutions. By applying these strategies, you can address objections effectively and increase the likelihood of receiving quality referrals for your business.

Finally, by effectively qualifying and following up on referrals, leveraging personalization and tailored messaging, and employing strategies to overcome common referral objections, you can maximize the conversion rate of your referral leads.

Rewarding and Recognizing Referral Partners

One of the area's most neglected often is the importance of rewarding and recognizing referral partners—the individuals or organizations that consistently refer business to you. Therefore the process of designing referral programs and incentives, providing meaningful rewards and recognition, and fostering a mutually beneficial relationship with your referral sources is an important area. By implementing effective strategies in this area, you can cultivate strong relationships with your referral partners and encourage ongoing referrals.

Designing referral programs and incentives: A well-designed referral program provides structure and motivation for your referral sources to actively refer business to you. By offering attractive incentives and clear guidelines, you can encourage and incentivize your referral partners to refer with enthusiasm.

Example: An online marketplace for handmade crafts and artwork establishes a referral program for their artists and artisans. They offer a tiered incentive structure, where artists receive a percentage of the sales generated from their referred customers. Additionally, they provide exclusive marketing opportunities and promotional features for artists who consistently refer high-value customers. This program motivates the artists to actively promote the platform and refer their network, leading to a steady influx of new sellers and buyers.

Providing meaningful rewards and recognition: Beyond monetary incentives, providing meaningful rewards and recognition is crucial for fostering a sense of appreciation and loyalty among your referral partners. Acknowledging their contributions and publicly recognizing their efforts can go a long way in strengthening the relationship.

Example: A software company implements a referral recognition program, where they regularly showcase their top referral partners on their website and social media channels. They highlight the success stories of these partners and the impact they have had on the company's growth. Additionally, the company hosts an annual referral partner appreciation event, where they invite their top advocates for an exclusive networking and recognition opportunity. These gestures of appreciation not only motivate the referral partners to continue referring but also inspire others to become active advocates.

Fostering a mutually beneficial relationship with referral sources: To maintain a strong referral network, it is important to foster a mutually beneficial relationship with your referral sources. By providing support, resources, and reciprocation, you can nurture a partnership that is advantageous for both parties involved.

Example: A business consultant regularly connects with their referral partners to understand their goals and challenges. They provide educational resources, such as industry reports and research findings, to help their partners stay informed and enhance their own knowledge base. Additionally, the consultant actively seeks opportunities to refer their partners to their network, introducing them to potential clients or collaborators. This mutual support and reciprocation strengthen the relationship, resulting in a consistent flow of referrals for the consultant and business growth for their partners.

By designing referral programs and incentives, providing meaningful rewards and recognition, and fostering a mutually beneficial relationship with your referral sources, you can cultivate a strong network of advocates who actively refer business to you.

Leveraging Technology for Referral Generation

In this chapter, we will look at the power of technology in enhancing your referral generation efforts- the utilization of Customer Relationship Management (CRM) systems for tracking and managing referrals, leveraging social media and online platforms for referral outreach, and the use of automation tools and software to streamline your referral processes. By harnessing the capabilities of technology, you can maximize your efficiency and effectiveness in generating and managing referrals.

Utilizing CRM systems for tracking and managing referrals: A CRM system is a valuable tool for organizing and tracking your referral activities. It enables you to capture and store important information about your referral sources, track the progress of referrals, and maintain a comprehensive view of your referral pipeline.

Example: A financial advisory firm integrates a CRM system into their operations to track and manage referrals. They create a dedicated referral source field in their CRM, allowing them to easily identify and segment contacts who have referred clients in the past. They set up automated reminders and follow-up tasks to ensure timely communication with referral sources and seamless tracking of referral progress. The CRM system enables them to monitor the success rate of referrals, identify trends, and make data-driven decisions to optimize their referral generation strategies.

Leveraging social media and online platforms for referral outreach: Social media and online platforms provide excellent avenues for reaching a broader audience and engaging with potential referral sources. By utilizing these platforms strategically, you can expand your referral network and increase your visibility among relevant communities.

Example: A marketing agency actively engages on social media platforms like LinkedIn and Twitter to build relationships with potential referral sources. They share valuable content related to their industry, such as marketing tips, case studies, and thought leadership articles. Through active participation in relevant online communities, they establish themselves as experts and attract the attention of potential referral partners, who are more likely to refer their services to their network.

Automation tools and software for streamlining referral processes: Automation tools and software can streamline your referral processes, saving time and improving efficiency. From referral tracking and reminders to personalized referral request templates, these tools can help you manage your referrals effectively.

Example: A real estate brokerage utilizes an automation tool specifically designed for referral management. The tool allows them to track referral sources, automate referral request emails, and set up customized workflows for referral follow-ups. It also generates reports and analytics to measure the success of their referral efforts. By leveraging automation, the brokerage streamlines their referral processes, ensuring consistent communication and increasing the likelihood of converting referrals into clients.

By utilizing CRM systems for tracking and managing referrals, leveraging social media and online platforms for referral outreach, and incorporating automation tools and software to streamline your referral processes, you can enhance your efficiency, effectiveness, and scalability in generating and managing referrals. In the subsequent chapters, we will explore advanced techniques and emerging technologies that can further optimize your referral generation efforts and drive sustained business growth.

Measuring and Scaling Referral Success

We will now focus on measuring and scaling your referral success, by covering the key metrics for evaluating referral performance, analyzing and optimizing your referral program, and strategies for scaling and expanding your referral network. By effectively measuring and scaling your referral efforts, you can maximize the impact of your referral program and drive substantial business growth.

Key metrics for evaluating referral performance: Measuring the performance of your referral program is crucial to understanding its effectiveness and identifying areas for improvement. By tracking key metrics, you can assess the success of your program and make data-driven decisions to optimize your referral generation strategies.

Example: An e-commerce company tracks the following key metrics to evaluate their referral performance:

Referral Conversion Rate: The percentage of referred leads that convert into customers.

Average Revenue per Referral: The average amount of revenue generated from each referral.

Referral Source Lifetime Value: The total revenue generated by customers referred by each source over their lifetime. By monitoring these metrics, the company can identify top-performing referral sources, assess the quality of referrals, and focus on optimizing their program to increase conversion rates and maximize customer lifetime value.

Here are some Key metrics for evaluating your referral performances:

When evaluating the performance of your referral program, it's essential to track key metrics that provide insights into its effectiveness. Here are eight key metrics for evaluating referral performance:

1. Referral Conversion Rate: This metric measures the percentage of referred leads that convert into customers. It helps you assess the quality of referrals and the effectiveness of your referral program. For example, if you receive 100 referrals and 20 of them become customers, your referral conversion rate would be 20%.

2. Referral Engagement Rate: The referral engagement rate measures the level of engagement and interaction from referred leads. It indicates how interested and active they are in your offerings. For instance, if 50% of referred leads open the referral email and click on the provided link, your referral engagement rate would be 50%.

3. Customer Lifetime Value (CLV) of Referred Customers: CLV measures the total revenue generated by referred customers over their entire lifecycle. Comparing the CLV of referred customers with other customer segments helps you determine the long-term value of referrals. For example, if referred customers have an average CLV of $5,000, while non-referred customers have an average CLV of $3,000, it shows the added value of referrals.

4. Referral Participation Rate: This metric measures the percentage of your customer base or target audience actively participating

in your referral program. It provides insights into the program's reach and engagement. For instance, if 10% of your customers actively participate in referring others, your referral participation rate would be 10%.

5. Referral Source Performance: Helps track the performance of different referral sources to identify the most effective channels or advocates and helps measure the number of referrals and conversion rates generated by each source. For example, if your top-performing referral source is a particular partner who consistently refers high-quality leads, it highlights their effectiveness.

6. Referral Program ROI: Calculate the return on investment (ROI) of your referral program by comparing the program's costs (including incentives, software, and resources) to the revenue generated from referred customers. This metric helps assess the financial impact and profitability of your referral program. For instance, if your referral program costs $10,000, and it generates $50,000 in revenue, your ROI would be 400%.

7. Referral Velocity: Referral velocity measures the speed at which referrals are generated and converted into customers. It helps you understand the efficiency and effectiveness of your referral program. For example, if you typically receive and convert referrals within a week, you have a high referral velocity.

8. Referral Feedback and Satisfaction: Collect feedback and satisfaction ratings from both referrers and referred customers. This qualitative data provides insights into their

experience, level of satisfaction, and areas for improvement. For example, if you receive positive feedback from referrers about the ease of the referral process and high satisfaction ratings from referred customers, it indicates a well-performing program.

Tracking these key metrics will enable you to evaluate the success and impact of your referral program, identify areas for improvement, and make data-driven decisions to optimize your program's performance.

Analyzing and optimizing your referral program: Analyzing and optimizing your referral program involves regularly reviewing and fine-tuning its components to ensure optimal performance. By analyzing referral data, gathering feedback, and implementing improvements, you can enhance the effectiveness and efficiency of your program.

Example: A software-as-a-service (SaaS) company regularly conducts surveys and gathers feedback from their customers and referral partners. Through this feedback, they identify areas of improvement, such as streamlining the referral process, providing additional resources to support advocates, and optimizing the referral incentives. By making data-driven changes based on customer and partner feedback, the company continually refines their referral program to increase engagement, referrals, and conversions.

Here are some Key ways of Analyzing and optimizing referral programs

1. Analyzing and optimizing referral programs is crucial for maximizing their effectiveness. Track Referral Channel Performance: Identify which referral channels are generating the

most successful referrals. Analyze data on referral sources such as email campaigns, social media platforms, partner networks, or customer advocacy programs. Optimize your program by focusing on the channels that drive the highest quality and quantity of referrals.

2. Analyze Referral Conversion Funnel: Evaluate the different stages of your referral conversion funnel, from initial referral acquisition to conversion into customers. Identify any bottlenecks or drop-off points in the process. Optimize the funnel by addressing barriers and streamlining the referral journey to increase conversion rates.

3. Monitor Referral Program KPIs: Continuously monitor key performance indicators (KPIs) related to your referral program, such as referral conversion rate, referral engagement rate, and referral participation rate. Regularly review these metrics to identify trends, patterns, and areas for improvement.

4. A/B Test Referral Program Elements: AB testing, also known as split testing is a comparison between two versions- involves comparing two versions of your marketing asset based on changing one element. Conduct A/B tests to experiment with different elements of your referral program. Test variables such as referral incentives, messaging, calls-to-action, landing pages, or referral program placement. By testing different variations, you can identify what drives higher engagement and conversion rates.

5. Solicit Feedback from Referrers and Referred Customers: Gather feedback from referrers and referred customers to understand their experiences with the referral program. Use surveys, interviews, or feedback forms to gather insights on what worked well and what can be improved. Use this feedback to optimize your program based on their suggestions and pain points.

6. Analyze Referral Program Costs: Evaluate the costs associated with running your referral program, including incentives, software, and marketing materials. Compare these costs with the revenue generated from referrals to assess the program's profitability. Optimize your program by finding a balance between incentivizing referrers and managing costs effectively.

7. Segment Referral Performance: Segment your referral program performance based on various factors such as customer demographics, referral sources, or referral types. Analyze performance across different segments to identify opportunities for targeted optimization. For example, if you find that a specific demographic group generates higher-quality referrals, you can tailor your messaging and targeting accordingly.

8. Benchmark against Industry Standards: Research industry benchmarks and best practices for referral programs. Compare your program's performance against these benchmarks to identify areas where you may be falling behind or excelling. Use the insights

to make informed decisions and optimize your program accordingly.

By utilizing these strategies, you can gain valuable insights into your referral program's performance, identify areas for optimization, and make data-driven decisions to enhance the program's effectiveness and drive greater results.

Scaling and expanding your referral network: Scaling your referral program involves expanding your network of referral sources and leveraging their collective power to generate a steady stream of referrals. By implementing strategies to attract new advocates and nurture existing ones, you can scale your referral network and drive significant business growth.

Example: A fitness studio develops a partner program where they collaborate with local wellness businesses, such as nutritionists, yoga studios, and athletic apparel stores. They offer mutual referrals, joint marketing initiatives, and exclusive discounts to each other's customers. By forging partnerships with complementary businesses, the fitness studio expands its reach and taps into new referral sources, increasing their potential customer base and revenue.

By measuring key metrics, analyzing and optimizing your referral program, and scaling and expanding your referral network, you can ensure the sustained success and growth of your referral program. In the subsequent chapters, we will explore advanced strategies and emerging trends that can further elevate your referral generation efforts, enabling you to unlock the full potential of referral-based business growth.

Overcoming Common Challenges and Obstacles

Sometimes you will encounter challenges and obstacles, like skepticism and resistance to providing referrals, and having to deal with unsuccessful or non-referred leads. So we will cover a few strategies for continuous improvement and adaptation- by proactively addressing these challenges, you can strengthen your referral program and maintain consistent business growth.

Addressing skepticism and resistance to referrals: Some individuals or organizations may express skepticism or resistance towards referrals, either due to a lack of trust or a preference for other marketing methods. It is essential to address these concerns and demonstrate the value and benefits of referrals.

Example: A marketing agency encounters a prospect who is skeptical about the effectiveness of referrals and prefers traditional advertising methods. To address this skepticism, the agency shares case studies and success stories of clients who have achieved significant results through referral-based marketing. They explain how referrals tap into the power of personal recommendations and trust, highlighting the cost-effectiveness and higher conversion rates of referrals compared to traditional advertising. By providing tangible evidence and addressing objections, the agency can alleviate the prospect's skepticism and open the door for a referral-based partnership.

Dealing with unsuccessful or non-referred leads: Not all leads generated through referrals will result in successful conversions. It is important to have strategies in place for handling unsuccessful or non-referred leads, ensuring that you maintain a positive relationship and explore alternative opportunities.

Example: A software company receives a referral for a potential client, but after engaging with the lead, they realize it is not an ideal fit for their product. Instead of abruptly ending the conversation, they take the time to understand the prospect's needs and challenges. They provide alternative recommendations, such as suggesting other software solutions or referring the prospect to another company in their network that may be a better fit. By demonstrating a genuine interest in helping the prospect, even if it does not lead to immediate business, they leave a positive impression and increase the likelihood of future referrals or potential partnerships.

Strategies for continuous improvement and adaptation: Referral programs require ongoing evaluation and adaptation to stay relevant and effective. By continually seeking feedback, analyzing data, and experimenting with new approaches, you can drive continuous improvement and ensure the long-term success of your referral program.

Example: A financial advisory firm regularly conducts surveys to gather feedback from their clients and referral partners. Based on the feedback received, they identify areas for improvement, such as streamlining their referral process, enhancing the referral incentives, or introducing new referral channels. They also closely monitor industry trends and changes in customer preferences to adapt their referral program accordingly. By embracing a culture of continuous improvement and adaptation, the firm stays ahead of the curve and maintains a competitive edge in generating and leveraging referrals.

By addressing skepticism and resistance to referrals, effectively handling unsuccessful or non-referred leads, and implementing strategies for continuous improvement and adaptation, you can overcome common challenges and obstacles that may arise in the referral generation process.

Testimonials and the Power of it!

If you've really provided great service, you are likely to receive a host of thankful messages and glowing praises from satisfied clients. But don't just keep them without using these effectively! You can use these as great testimonials and rave about your service for others to note.

Human beings by nature will not do business with anyone they perceive to be untrustworthy, and therefore often turn to others, especially people like them with the same challenges and pain points, for advice on the trustworthiness of anything, particularly for large investments like properties, vehicles, appliances etc.

In key surveys carried out by agencies there has been enough and more evidence to demonstrate the power of online reviews and testimonials in establishing trust:

- ✓ *97% of consumers surveyed searched for a local business online*
- ✓ *73% said positive reviews made them trust local businesses more*
- ✓ *85% of those surveyed said they trust online reviews as much as personal recommendations*
- ✓ *Consumers read an average of seven reviews before they trust and move on to do a business*
- ✓ *Agents with 10 or more reviews see a 300% increase in listings versus agents with no reviews.*

- ✓ *And according to Placester.com **85% of all consumers use reviews to decide on purchases.***
- ✓ *They all trust peer recommendations six more times than a normal advertisement.*

Testimonials therefore are powerful trust signals that can go a long way in enticing new clients to your business. They are powerful tools that you/ your organization can use in turning around an unhappy customer or proving the credibility of your service. Client testimonials are just as important as word-of-mouth recommendations, and they play a vital role in helping you build trust with your potential clients.

Staying engaged and maintaining a good relationship with your clients even after a sale will make it easier to request for reviews, testimonials and referrals. If you've never requested a testimonial, it's not too late to start! You can start building your testimonial library by reaching out to clients you've worked with in the last few months and going forward from there, establish a process for collecting feedback and a testimonial from each and every client you serve.

We recommend that sales professionals always carry a 'Customer Feedback Book' with them, and as you reach this stage where you know that the client is elated, then this is the time to bring the book out and have the customer write a few lines on what they felt about you, your service, your attitude, helpfulness etc.

Though testimonials have immense value on your website, you can no doubt use them to attract clients in other ways as well. A testimonial is one of the best gifts a sales person can receive. Testimonials are words and experiences from past clients and customers sharing their transaction experiences.

How Powerful are Testimonials?

- ✓ Sales people are usually looked at as a distrusted profession: Many people are put off by their pushy approach and therefore this profession is much disliked. Hence the need for you as a 'professional' sales person is to carry sufficient proof and evidence of who you really are. And who is the best person to say so? Customers who have already experienced your service!

- ✓ Testimonials build credibility and trust: The most obvious and most important reason to add testimonials to your website or carry them on calls is that they build credibility. Testimonials make all the difference for a sales professionals' credibility. Obviously, anyone selling their services would say they deliver a great experience; but it's much more believable when we hear it from others who have seen and experienced it firsthand!

- ✓ They have the power to make or break a deal: If they aren't up to standard (or if they are absent altogether) customers will be susceptible to doubt. Sales professionals without the outspoken support of their past clients are at a massive disadvantage.

- ✓ Happy customers are the most valuable advocates for your business: Nothing creates trust as well as testimonials from previous customers who are able to tell that you were professional and trustworthy, and that the entire process went smoothly. Other people are more likely to believe the words of actual customers than what you say in advertisements and other branded content.

✓ Draws on emotions quickly: When people who are struggling, see their experience and feelings reflected back to them in a testimonial, then reading about that satisfied client's happy ending, allows the potential client to want to come to you to have the same joyful experience

✓ A Good Story is EVERYTHING: Your testimonials should be centered on a good story. By having good characters (past clients), with a problem (conflict), and how you helped them with their solution (resolution) these stories tap into our brains, pulling us into the plot, wanting more. This is how we relate with the world. And this is why good testimonials draw in your prospects and connect with them emotionally.

✓ Customers love being featured: By obtaining a testimonial, not only are you asking for their honest opinion after your transaction is finished, but you're also showing them how much their thoughts matter to you when you post them on your website or show them off to others. In fact most will actually be thrilled to see their words or even photos go live on your website!

✓ Requesting testimonials encourages referrals: Having your happy clients write out what they appreciated about your service brings it to the front of their minds and will make it that much easier for them to bring you up when people compliment their gorgeous purchase.

- ✓ Testimonials can be used long term: Having a bank of strong testimonials boosts marketing efforts and can go a long way as it doesn't matter how old they are.
- ✓ The Process will help you do a self-check and grow: Because some large purchases are so emotionally-charged, you might not therefore always result in a noteworthy conversation, but sometimes clients are itching to share praise and constructive criticism, as not everyone will be prepared to give a beautiful testimonial, but the opportunity to hear your clients' reflections and sift through them for actionable and helpful criticisms is a gift and a helpful tool in itself.
- ✓ Testimonials helps boost SEO: Adding testimonials to your website can help ensure it ranks high when searches are carried out on the internet.

Remember that your customer's testimonials are much more effective than your own content and advertisements and in order to obtain such testimonials, you need to provide unmatched customer service so that your clients are willing to recommend you.

So how do you get them?

- ✓ Be Worthy of Praise: The first and most important rule to getting testimonials is to **be worth it.** You can't expect your customers to tell how much they trust you and how well the buying process went off if that is not true and the best way to find out if your customers are happy is to ask for feedback. If the feedback is positive, then you have a great chance that

they would be willing to give a testimonial and do it right way
- ✓ Ask: If you do not ask, you do not get- it is as simple as that. And it is best done face-to-face- as sending an email or message may have them forgetting about it or wanting to do it later
- ✓ Choose the medium: Testimonials can come in different forms: written, audio or video,
- ✓ Questions to ask: *"If you've been happy with my service would you like to give me few lines on what you felt about it"* or *"How would you describe the process and experience with me/ our team?"*
- ✓ Make it quick and easy: Most people do not like spending time writing, especially a testimonial. This is why we recommend carrying a 'Customer Feedback Book' or sheets of 'Customer Feedback Forms' so that you could open up the same at the right time and have them quickly jot down a few sentences.
- ✓ Make immediate use of these testimonials: After you have your testimonials you need to use them effectively and featuring these testimonials on your website and social media is a good start as it will help prospective customers that land on your website or any social media page, to see the recommendations from your previous customers.

What should an ideal Client Testimonial include?

Usually great testimonials cover some of these key elements below:

- ✓ Must have specific information: How did you as the sales professional help them take a decision?
- ✓ Must be authentic: The testimonial must allow the clients genuine thoughts and personality to shine through the testimonial making others get the sense of how unique the experience was. This can include anything from the fact that you as the sales professional helped them decide on say a set of dining furniture to fit in into their new home or of how you negotiated a fantastic deal to close in early on their dream home.
- ✓ Must be thorough: This is an essential item - being thorough in the review will allow other consumers to connect with you as their advisor, knowing precisely what they will get as a buyer. Thoroughness includes telling future consumers the events leading up to the sale, how the process went from start to finish, and everything you did to help them along the way.
- ✓ Must emphasize the benefits: It must convey to the world how amazing it was to work with you as their advisor and how you made the entire transaction process simple and efficient. How it was such a pleasure to work with you must be said in the review.

Remember: As a Sales Professional, this is your most powerful tool- So make the best use of every opportunity to your advantage!

Bonus: Networking Skills

What is Networking?
The action of interacting with others to exchange information, ideas, and resources and develop contacts/ referrals which can be for mutual benefit. This is another great way to building referrals and contacts.

Why Network?
75% - 80% of business is obtained as a direct result of some sort of networking. There is some truth in the old saying: "It is not what you know, but who you know."
Networking is the key to your business success

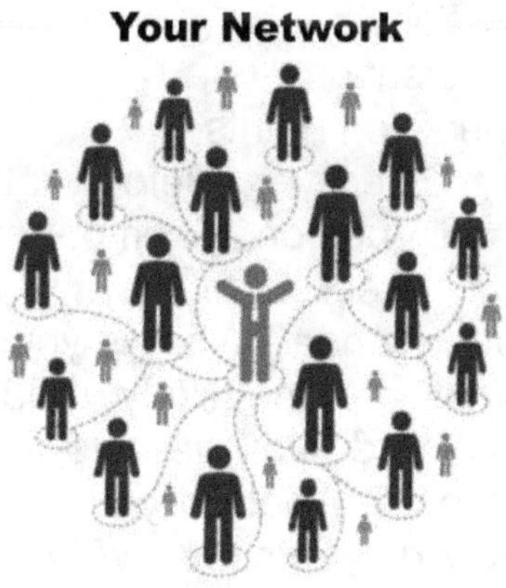

What are the main benefits of Networking?
- ✓ Access to knowledge through contacts
- ✓ Develop contacts that can provide with support and advice
- ✓ Learn from other people
- ✓ Create collaborations

- ✓ Can create otherwise unknown chances for collaboration and new opportunities.
- ✓ Development of your emotional and creative intelligence though added support and advice, including the support from mentors and champions
- ✓ Exposure to new environments
- ✓ Increase your confidence

The Key Steps to Networking Successfully

The best place to network is to begin in your comfort zone

Step 1: Your Comfort Zone: Your comfort zone will be in the areas you know, namely: what you want, who and where you are

- ✓ Your Agenda
- ✓ Your Story
- ✓ Your Questions
- ✓ Your Conversations
- ✓ Your Connection Points

Step 2: Your Objective: Before attempting to network-online or in-person, it's important to resolve in your mind the question of why. Why are doing this? What's your agenda? What is your objective of networking? What are the likely groups that you could get into? Who do you need to talk to? Target people/organizations? What do you want to achieve or find out? Where do you hope it will lead you?

How could you contact them?

- ✓ Looking up their profile
- ✓ Networking at events
- ✓ Asking connections

Step 3: Make a start by joining the Networking Groups you decided on in the earlier step. One recommended way to begin networking is to join at least two organizations. One networking group related to your target market and another of your peers. The target market group will allow you to meet people who you would like to work with and promote your business, whereas the peer group is for gathering knowledge in your field by hanging out with others like yourself.

Step 4: Do your Preparation (This step is very important)

Write down who you need to talk to, and why you want to talk to them.

Consider also, what do you want to find out? Or where would you like this to lead?

In other words, it's important to know your purpose - and in doing so you can increase your satisfaction levels afterwards.

You must have a compelling Story: Your Elevator Speech. How do you present yourself in different contexts? And this can often be the most difficult part of any event – how to introduce yourself to strangers. Your goal should be something like:

1. Introduce yourself to the people in your core group – these can simply be the people near you in a lecture or virtual breakout room. Try and find a connection point. Did you once work with one of their collaborators, mentors or trainees? Your aim should be that they remember meeting you.

2. Ensure that people in this core group know what specialty and industry you are in. Prepare your specific 'attention-grabbing' statements to answer the questions "Who are you and what do you do?"

Preparing a "story" (Elevator Speech or if you like a "statement of purpose") in advance will greatly help you settle in and take that first networking step.

Do your Homework on the Networking Group/ Event!

Things to do BEFORE the networking meeting or event:

1. Get a list of attendees
   - ✓ Ask the host or facilitator
   - ✓ Enquire online
2. Search for attendee's websites
   - ✓ Gather information
   - ✓ Review company services
   - ✓ Look at their picture
3. Select the people you want to meet
   - ✓ Write down their names
   - ✓ Call them before the event
   - ✓ Seek them out at the event
4. Ask the host or facilitator to introduce you to 2 or 3 people
   - ✓ People who would typically be a referral source
   - ✓ People who may be a potential client
   - ✓ People who are mover's and shaker's

Think about:
- ✓ What do you want to find more out about?
- ✓ How are you going to bring these questions into conversations?

Things to bring to the meeting or event:
- ✓ Have plenty of business cards with you (at least 50)
- ✓ Place business cards in your left pocket
- ✓ Name badges (if applicable)

Things to DO at the meeting or event:
- ✓ Get there early and stay late
- ✓ Introduce yourself within 60 seconds of entering the room

Step 5: What Impression do you want to create: Your first 30 Seconds Count!

"You only get one chance to make a <u>first</u> good impression."

First Impressions

- ✓ Dress for the Occasion: 60% of people are visual communicators. This means that to 60% of the world-image is key.
- ✓ Demeanor: Business entrance should be professional and quite seamless and understated.
- ✓ Introductions: Person of higher rank receives the introduction. Use the name of higher-ranking person first.
- ✓ Handshake and Share Business Card

Step 6: Working your way around in the Event

1. Meet new contacts
- ✓ Do not hang with people you know
- ✓ Meet people you want to do business with
- ✓ It is not a card gathering experience
2. Look for groups of 2 or 3 people
- ✓ Get into groups already formed
- ✓ An easy way to introduce yourself to a group is *"Do you mind if I join your conversation?"*
- ✓ If approaching a speaker or any other group official have something relevant to ask e.g. *'I thought X part of your paper was really interesting, in particular I wanted to ask about...'*
3. Seek information first
- ✓ Get others to reveal their wants and needs
- ✓ Let others shine and feel good about themselves
- ✓ Make others believe that you are listening and are interested
- ✓ Look at the other person for approximately 60% of the time. Give plenty of eye-contact

but be careful not to make them feel uncomfortable.

✓ When listening, nod and make encouraging sounds and gestures.

✓ Use the other person's name early in the conversation. This is not only seen as polite but will also reinforce the name in your mind so you are less likely to forget it!

✓ Smile!

✓ Try to ask the other person open questions (the type of questions that require more than a yes or no answer).

✓ Avoid contentious topics of conversation.

✓ Use feedback to summarize, reflect and clarify back to the other person what you think they have said. This gives opportunity for any misunderstandings to be rectified quickly.

✓ Talk about things that refer back to what the other person has said. Find links between common experiences.

4. Give your "elevator speech"

✓ Reveal how you can help them

✓ Briefly explain what you do and how you do it

✓ Build their curiosity and interest in you

5. Conversation conclusions

✓ If you want to do business, conclude your conversation with offers and requests

✓ Send follow-up materials

✓ Introduce them to a colleague

✓ Ask for a business card

• Say something like *"It seems as though it would be worth following up with a more specific discussion. Would you be open to meeting up after the conference?"* or *"I will call you tomorrow and see if we can help each other, okay?"* If they agree to a meeting see if you can schedule it right then and there with your phone and ask if they have theirs.

6. If you do not want to do business, conclude your conversation:

- Do not exchange business cards
- Use *the great escape* exit: *"I have enjoyed meeting you and I look forward to seeing you again."*
- Or to make a graceful exit. *"I have to make a quick call"*, or *"I'm going to get a drink of water if you'd excuse me?"* or *"I just spotted someone else I need to speak to, lovely to meet you."* or *"I've enjoyed meeting you. I know you have others you would like to meet and so would I . . . ."*

Step 7: After the Event

Take time to write notes on the back of (their) business card or by using the Contacts App on your phone.

Review notes you have made

1. Write a quick note or send an email: remind them that you met them at the event and what you spoke about.
   ✓ Send it soon after the event (within 24 hours)
   ✓ Keep it simple and friendly
2. Send an article or useful resource
   ✓ Relevant article, important telephone number or website
   ✓ Make sure it is simple and helpful
3. Send a thank-you note for suggestions, ideas, and resources resulting from your contact. Show appreciation
4. Do them a favor

- ✓ Introduce them to associates, clients and vendors
- ✓ Help them to achieve their goals
5. Send them a referral. Ask for a follow-up call
6. Send a gift
- ✓ Make it appropriate
- ✓ Always add a note
7. Keep contacts on your mailing list
- ✓ Use contact management software for tracking
- ✓ Persistence pays

Name Placement Tags or Badges

Name badges are always worn on the right hand side of your front shoulder area. Why? The reason is that as you extend your hand in greeting, the gaze of the person you are meeting can easily follow your extended arm back allowing for a natural progression for the eyes to the name tag.

Some other good tips include:
- ✓ Arrive early. Arriving before the venue is noisy and full of people lets you get accustomed to the sights and sounds of the room before they become overwhelming. You can also scope out places to retreat to if you need a moment of solitude.
- ✓ Arrive with a friend or colleague. Not knowing anyone can be uncomfortable. Walking in with a friend guarantees you will know at least one person in the room who can introduce you to others.
- ✓ Have strategies to re-energize mid-event. Give yourself a networking time limit and then go somewhere to regroup in solitude. Or consider taking a break to peruse the display

items on the shelf or elsewhere. Sometimes you just need to be seen and not heard.

Rules for Business Introductions

- ✓ Know the status and rank
- ✓ Know the first and last names
- ✓ Pronounce each person's name correctly
- ✓ Know some piece of relative information
- ✓ Knowledge of person's job
- ✓ Use formal, academic or political title before last name
- ✓ Mr., Mrs., or Ms.
- ✓ Use formal introductions for senior-ranking executives
- ✓ Repeat person's name
- ✓ Name Tags do not replace proper introductions

And Finally…Some Deadly Networking Mistakes

- ✓ Hanging around your friends
- ✓ Staying too long in one group
- ✓ Being too busy eating and drinking
- ✓ Talking nonstop
- ✓ Asking about the weather or other irrelevant topics
- ✓ Getting pushy about meeting socially
- ✓ No follow-up or follow-through

The Future of Referral-Based Selling

In this final chapter, we will explore the future of referral-based selling and the trends, emerging technologies, evolving customer behaviors, and the need for adaptation in a rapidly changing sales landscape. Understanding and embracing these changes will position you for continued success in generating and leveraging referrals.

Trends and emerging technologies in referral generation: Referral generation is not immune to the advancements of technology and evolving market trends. Staying abreast of these trends and leveraging emerging technologies can significantly enhance your referral program's effectiveness.

For example, with the rise of influencer marketing, businesses are leveraging influencers to generate referrals. They partner with influencers who have a relevant audience and engage them in promoting their products or services, thus tapping into the influencers' trusted recommendations to drive referrals.

Evolving customer behaviors and preferences: Customer behaviors and preferences continually evolve, driven by changes in technology and societal shifts. Understanding these changes is crucial for adapting your referral strategies to meet the evolving needs and expectations of your customers.

For example, the preference for Online Referral Platforms: Customers are increasingly relying on online platforms and review sites to seek referrals and recommendations. Businesses need to optimize their online presence and actively manage their reputation on these platforms to attract and leverage customer referrals effectively.

Adapting to a rapidly changing sales landscape: The sales landscape is continuously evolving, with new sales methodologies and approaches emerging. Adapting to these changes and adopting innovative sales techniques is vital to remain competitive and successful in the referral-based selling arena.

For example-Social Selling: Sales professionals are increasingly leveraging social media platforms to build relationships, engage with potential referral partners, and establish credibility. By actively participating in relevant online communities, sharing valuable content, and nurturing relationships, sales professionals can position themselves as trusted experts and attract referrals from their network.

As the future unfolds, embracing emerging technologies, understanding evolving customer behaviors and preferences, and adapting to the rapidly changing sales landscape will be critical for the success of your referral-based selling efforts. By staying ahead of the curve and proactively adjusting your strategies, you can position yourself as a leader in referral generation and leverage the full potential of this powerful sales technique.

In conclusion, the power of sales referrals is undeniable, and their impact on business growth is substantial. By understanding the concept of sales referrals, harnessing the benefits they offer, and implementing effective strategies to generate and leverage referrals, you can create a self-sustaining referral ecosystem that fuels your business growth. With the future in mind, it is crucial to stay agile, embrace emerging trends and technologies, and continuously adapt your referral program to meet the evolving needs of your customers and the dynamic sales landscape. By doing so, you will position yourself for sustained success and ongoing business growth through the power of sales referrals.

Conclusion: Unlocking the Power of Sales Referrals

Congratulations! You have journeyed through the comprehensive exploration of the power of sales referrals. Having concluded your journey through this book, remember that unlocking the full potential of sales referrals is an ongoing process. Here are some final points to keep in mind:

1. Commitment and Consistency: Generating and leveraging referrals requires commitment and consistency. Make referrals an integral part of your sales strategy and ensure everyone in your organization understands their value.

2. Relationships are Key: Focus on building and nurturing relationships, both with your customers and referral sources. Actively engage with them, provide exceptional experiences, and demonstrate your appreciation for their referrals.

3. Embrace Technology and Innovation: Leverage technology to streamline your referral processes, track and manage referrals, and stay connected with your network. Stay updated on emerging technologies and innovative approaches to stay ahead of the competition.

4. Measure and Optimize: Continuously measure and optimize your referral program. Track key metrics, gather feedback, and make data-driven decisions to enhance your program's effectiveness.

5. Evolve with Customer Behaviors: Stay attuned to evolving customer behaviors and preferences. Adapt your referral strategies to align with their changing needs and the digital landscape they inhabit.
6. Seek Collaboration and Learning Opportunities: Engage with industry peers, attend conferences, and join communities focused on sales and referrals. Collaborate and learn from others' experiences to expand your knowledge and refine your approach.

Remember, referrals are not just a one-time event but a continuous process. By cultivating a referral mindset, nurturing relationships, providing exceptional experiences, and embracing technology, you can unlock the full potential of sales referrals and experience sustainable business growth.

Thank you for embarking on this journey to unlock the power of sales referrals. As you apply the knowledge and strategies shared in this book, may you thrive in generating and leveraging referrals, and may your business reach new heights of success. Best of luck on your referral-driven journey!

About the Author
'GERARD ASSEY'

Gerard Assey is a Graduate in Economics, a PGD in Management (HRD) and holds a Doctorate in Leadership. Gerard holds several International Qualifications in Sales, Debt Collection, Training & Teaching, and is a 'Fellow' of the prestigious 'Institute of Sales & Marketing Management'-UK, a Certified NLP Practitioner, a 'Certified Trainer', an 'Accredited Management Teacher-Behavioral Sciences', a 'Certified Competency Facilitator', a 'Certified Management Consultant'- (the International credentials of a professional management consultant, awarded in accordance with global standards of the ICMCI); and a Certification from the University of Michigan in 'Successful Negotiation: Essential Strategies and Skills'

He is also a Member of the 'National Association of Sales Professionals' backed with several years experience in varied industries, both in India and Overseas. He also holds an 'Etiquette Consultant' Certification from the USA (by Sue Fox, Author of Best Seller: 'Business Etiquette for Dummies'. She has trained some of the top celebrities' world over). He was also a recipient of a scholarship for extensive training in Japan on 'Corporate Management for India'.

Gerard Assey is 'Founder & Chief Corporate Trainer' of the Group: **'Citius, Altius, Fortius Unlimited'**- an organization that **celebrated 20 years of Glorious Service** in 2021, focusing on 3 Core Competencies:

People. Performance. Profit; in functional areas of Sales & Marketing, HR & Organizational Development, covering Recruitment, Training & Consultancy!

Having managed organizations with large Sales Forces in India & Overseas, his specialization cover extensive areas of Sales Training (All levels - Presentation, Negotiation, Key/ Strategic Accounts Management & Managerial Skills for all sectors), Bid Proposal/ Capture Planning/ Management Trainings, Retail Sales, Customer Service & Customer Retention Programs, Training for Prevention & Collection of Debt, Self & Personal Development Programs (Time Management, Teamwork & Team Building, Business Etiquette & Personal Grooming, Leadership & Managerial Skills, People Management Skills, Train-the-Trainer etc), including preparation of Custom-designed Business Manuals for Internal (HR, Induction, and Sales etc) & External use (Instruction, User Manuals).

Gerard has successfully conducted over 5950 Trainings & Workshops (as of May '23) all across India, Middle East, Africa, Europe & S.E. Asia. Besides public programs conducted regularly, both in India & Overseas, he has some of the top names as clients whom he services from Single Owners to large Public & Government undertakings, covering all sectors, for their in-house needs.

His website: www.CollectionSkills.com is the only one in this part of the world to be featured in the 'Collections & Credit Risk Magazine-USA' under 'Who's Who in Training' and ranks TOP, along with other websites listed below on most search engines.

Gerard is author of 64 books already (June 2023),

A few of the business related books being:

1. Bite-sized Bits on Commonsense Management
2. Heart to Heart on Life's Principles'
3. How to become a Successful Manager
4. The Sales Professionals' Master Workbook of S.Y.S.T.E.M.S
5. The Professional Business Email Etiquette Handbook & Guide
6. The Professional Business Video-Conferencing Etiquette Handbook & Guide
7. Professional Presentation Skills
8. Exceptional Customer Service
9. Professional Tele-Marketing Skills
10. Professional Debt Collection Skills
11. The G.R.E.A.T. Sales & Service Workbook
12. Sales Training Advantage for Results (*The Ultimate Sales Training Manual to enable you stand out as a S.T.A.R.*)
13. CEO Daily Planner & Organizer
14. The Sales Professionals' Master Daily Planner
15. The Professional Debt Collector's Master Daily Planner
16. My Daily Planner & Organizer
17. MY EMERGENCY INFORMATION RECORD (Family Emergency & Peace of Mind Planner)
18. The Ultimate Therapist & Counselors Planner and Organizer
19. Building an Ethical Workplace
20. Managing Relationships at Work
21. Managing Business Meetings Effectively
22. Effective Delegation Skills
23. Goal Setting for Success
24. B2B Selling by Email
25. Professional Business Etiquette & Grooming
26. Dining Etiquette & Table Manners
27. Effective Networking Skills
28. Grooming, Etiquette & Manners for Teens, Young Adults & Future Leaders
29. Inter-Personal Skills
30. Get Ready, Get Hired!
31. Selling in a Recession
32. Effective Receivables Management in an Economic Downturn!
33. Real Estate & Property Sales Training
34. Credit Sales & Accounts Receivable Management
35. Selling Skills for Real Estate & Property Advisors
36. Take G.R.E.A.T. C.A.R.E!
37. Spa, Salon & Health Club Selling Skills
38. Selling Travel, Holiday & MICE Services
39. Selling Skills for Spa's, Salons & Health Clubs
40. Retailing in Salons & Spas
41. Selling Holiday, Vacation, Tours & Packages
42. The Power of Sales Referrals

Besides regularly contributing to business & trade journals, including international ones such as the 'Creative Training Techniques' and the 'Sales News' of the U.S.A, He is also a member of several prestigious bodies & trade associations, having participated in many Conferences & Workshops in India & Overseas.

Prior to his last assignment of leading & managing a large MNC as head, Gerard had a 3-year stint in the Middle East as a Consultant with a leading British Consultancy Firm.

As the past 'Official Country Representative' for the International Business Award- 'THE STEVIES'-(the business world's own Oscar) for about 4 years- he ensured a few Indian companies that qualify for the same every year!

Gerard can be contacted at:

Email: training@Sales-Training.in,training@CollectionSkills.com

Websites:

www.Sales-Training.in
www.EtiquetteWorks.in
www.CollectionSkills.com
www.RetailSalesTraining.in
www.SalesTrainingIndia.com
www.ManualPreparation.com
www.TrainingWithPuppets.com
www.FirstContactAcademy.com
www.SalesAndMarketingRecruiter.com

Our TRAININGS & BOOKS that can help your team

- ✓ **Sales Effectiveness**: Selling Skills for any Sector: Service/ Logistics/ FMCG Realty/ Insurance & Finance/ Media/ SPA's, Health Clubs & Salons/ Key Account Management, Effective Negotiation Skills/ Bid & Proposal Management Skills/ Retail Sales Training: Any Sector (Auto, Jewelry, Clothing, Luxury etc)
- ✓ **Customer Service Skills**-Complaints Handling & Customer Retention
- ✓ **Debt Prevention & Collection Skills**
- ✓ **Etiquette & Grooming**
- ✓ **Leadership & Managerial Skills**
- ✓ **Self & Personal Development Skills**: Presentation Skills/ Effective Communication Skills/Business Proposal Writing Skills/ Problem Solving & Decision Making Skills/ Empowering Secretaries-The perfect PA! (For Secretaries & PA's)/ Effective Time Management/ Teamwork & Teambuilding/ P.R.I.D.E- **P**ersonal **R**esponsibility **I**n **D**elivering **E**xcellence

A Few of Our Business Books
By the Top Corporate Trainer & Author of 64 Books! (June '23)
And...DAILY PLANNERS for Every Corporate Need!
All Books available Online on all leading Stores in E-book & Paperback Formats
Experts in Training for over 22 years:
Sales, Debt Prevention & Collection, Etiquette & Grooming ,
Leadership & Managerial Skills, Self & Personal Development Programs
By the Top Corporate Trainer (Over 5850 workshops) &
Author of 64 Published Books (June 23)